THE POWER OF THE
BR STANDARD PACIFICS

D1135625

Plate 1:   The Sunday down 'Mid-Day Scot' is in the charge of Britannia Pacific No. 70042 *Lord Roberts* **passing Shap Wells**
on the climb to Shap Summit on 26th July, 1964.

J.S. Whiteley

THE POWER OF THE
BR STANDARD
PACIFICS

by
J.S. Whiteley
&
G.W. Morrison

SBN 86093 067 X

Printed by B.H. Blackwell Ltd. in the City of Oxford

Published by
Oxford Publishing Co. Ltd., 8 The Roundway, Oxford

Plate 2: Beautifully turned out by Stewarts Lane depot, No. 70004 *William Shakespeare* is passing Bickley Junction on 13th September, 1952 heading the down 'Golden Arrow'.
B. Morrison

ACKNOWLEDGEMENTS

Once again it is the authors' pleasure to thank all the photographers who have kindly allowed inclusion of their pictures, and without whose help we would not have been able to include such a comprehensive pictorial record of the BR Standard Pacifics. Special thanks to John Holroyd for his help with the art work and to Margaret Morley for typing the manuscript.

Plate 3: The well proportioned lines of the Britannia Pacifics can be seen in this picture of No. 70020 *Mercury* at Newton Heath shed on 7th December, 1963.

G.W. Morrison

INTRODUCTION

When the first Britannia Pacific emerged from Crewe Works early in 1951, few people could have imagined that this class of 55 engines was destined to have a life of less than 18 years, and one member of the class would have the dubious honour of sharing the working of the last BR steam hauled train on the 11th August, 1968. The short life of these two-cylinder Class 7 engines was in no way attributable to poor performance, in fact some would suggest that they were the most successful of all Riddles standard designs and at times the equal of four-cylinder engines of class 8 power. They were designed to incorporate the most successful features of the locomotives of the four pre-nationalisation railways, and it is worth remembering that they were introduced as mixed traffic engines with coupled wheels of only 6′ 2″ diameter. In the event, they performed extremely well on express passenger duties on some very exacting routes, and it was only in their latter years that they were regularly to be found on freight workings in rather run down condition which was a hallmark of neglected steam power in the mid sixties. Two members of the class have, however, been preserved, No. 70000 *Britannia* which can be seen on the Severn Valley Railway at the time of writing, and No. 70013 *Oliver Cromwell* which is at Bressingham Museum.

Whilst the Britannias proved very successful, unfortunately the same could not be said of the Clans. These engines were a slightly scaled down version of the Britannias, with a smaller boiler and cylinders. Only ten were built at Crewe in 1951/2 and, although a further 15 were ordered for the Southern and Scottish Regions, the order was subsequently cancelled after the Modernisation Plan of 1955 was announced. They were shedded at Polmadie and Carlisle Kingmoor for the whole of their working lives and spent most of their time working on Glasgow, Manchester, Liverpool and Perth trains with the last one being withdrawn in May, 1966. Many considered them to be the most handsome of the standard designs and it is unfortunate that one has not been preserved.

The unique three-cylinder Class 8 BR Standard Pacific No. 71000 *Duke of Gloucester* was destined to have an even shorter working life than the Clans, emerging from Crewe in 1954 and being withdrawn from traffic only eight years later, at the end of 1962. Possibly by 1954 this engine was not really needed, and, due to a lack of study and development, it never distinguished itself. It is, however, being restored by the Main Line Steam Trust at Loughborough.

Such, then, is the brief history of the BR Standard Pacifics, and in this book can be seen the wide variety of their duties all over the country, ranging from such prestige workings as the Golden Arrow to the most mundane of freight duties.

J.S. Whiteley
February, 1979.

THE BRITANNIAS

Plate 4: No. 70011 *Hotspur* is being lowered on to its bogies in the erecting shops at Crewe Works in 1951.   *British Rail, London Midland Region.*

SUMMARY

BR No.	Name	Date Built	W/D	BR No.	Name	Date Built	W/D
70000	Britannia	1/51	5/66	70028	Royal Star	10/52	9/67
70001	Lord Hurcomb	2/51	9/66	70029	Shooting Star	11/52	10/67
70002	Geoffrey Chaucer	3/51	1/67	70030	William Wordsworth	11/52	6/66
70003	John Bunyan	3/51	3/67	70031	Byron	11/52	11/67
70004	William Shakespeare	3/51	12/67	70032	Tennyson	12/52	9/67
70005	John Milton	4/51	7/67	70033	Charles Dickens	12/52	7/67
70006	Robert Burns	4/51	5/67	70034	Thomas Hardy	12/52	5/67
70007	Coeur-de-Lion	4/51	6/65	70035	Rudyard Kipling	12/52	12/67
70008	Black Prince	4/51	1/67	70036	Boadicea	12/52	10/66
70009	Alfred the Great	5/51	1/67	70037	Hereward the Wake	12/52	11/66
70010	Owen Glendower	5/51	9/67	70038	Robin Hood	1/53	8/67
70011	Hotspur	5/51	12/67	70039	Sir Christopher Wren	2/53	9/67
70012	John of Gaunt	5/51	12/67	70040	Clive of India	3/53	4/67
70013	Oliver Cromwell	5/51	8/68	70041	Sir John Moore	3/53	4/67
70014	Iron Duke	6/51	12/67	70042	Lord Roberts	4/53	5/67
70015	Apollo	6/51	8/67	70043	Lord Kitchener	6/53	8/65
70016	Ariel	6/51	8/67	70044	Earl Haig	6/53	10/66
70017	Arrow	6/51	9/66	70045	Lord Rowallan	6/54	12/67
70018	Flying Dutchman	6/51	12/66	70046	Anzac	7/54	7/67
70019	Lightning	6/51	3/66	70047		7/54	7/67
70020	Mercury	7/51	1/67	70048	The Territorial Army		
70021	Morning Star	8/51	12/67		1908–1958	8/54	5/67
70022	Tornado	8/51	12/67	70049	Solway Firth	8/54	12/67
70023	Venus	8/51	12/67	70050	Firth of Clyde	8/54	8/66
70024	Vulcan	10/51	12/67	70051	Firth of Forth	8/54	12/67
70025	Western Star	9/52	12/67	70052	Firth of Tay	8/54	3/67
70026	Polar Star	10/52	1/67	70053	Moray Firth	9/54	4/67
70027	Rising Star	10/52	6/67	70054	Dornoch Firth	9/54	11/66

THE NORFOLKMAN

Plate 5: Right
No. 70000 *Britannia* emerged from Crewe works early in 1951 and was named at Marylebone on 30th January, 1951. The first fifteen engines of the class were for the Eastern Region in order to improve the services from Liverpool Street to East Anglia. *Britannia* is nearing Ingatestone heading the down 'Norfolkman', the 10.00 Liverpool Street—Norwich express on 7th April, 1951.   *R.E. Vincent*

Plate 6: Left
The Britannias were turned out in BR passenger green livery with orange and black lining. In this side view of *Britannia* taken on 26th February, 1951, shortly after entering service, the original small flat dome cover can be seen, together with the hollow axles on the coupled wheels which were later to prove troublesome and as a result were plugged.

R.E. Vincent

Plate 7: Below
No. 70002 *Geoffrey Chaucer* was one of the first eight Britannias which were all shedded at Stratford and shared in working the express services to East Anglia. It is heading the down 'Norfolkman' near Shenfield on 21st May, 1951 when only a few weeks old, but having the larger dome cover.

R.E. Vincent

NORWICH EXPRESSES

Plate 8: Left
The Britannias were very well received on the Great Eastern line and succeeded in transforming the services to East Anglia. No. 70035 *Rudyard Kipling* was one of the 1952 batch and was allocated to Norwich. On 31st August, 1957 it is picking up water on Ipswich troughs whilst heading the 14.45 Norwich–Liverpool Street express.
R.E. Vincent

Plate 9: Below
No. 70042 *Lord Roberts* was delivered in April 1953 and shedded at Stratford. By this time draught screens had been fitted between engine and tender as a result of crews complaining about the cabs being draughty. It is climbing Brentwood Bank on 5th September, 1953 heading a Liverpool Street–Norwich express.
B. Morrison

THE RED DRAGON

Plate 10: Above   Twenty-five Britannias were scheduled for the 1951 building programme, Nos. 70000—14 were intended for the Eastern Region and Nos. 70015—24 for the Western. In the event, however, Nos. 70009/14 were sent on loan to the Southern and Nos. 70015/16 to the London Midland for promotional purposes. The eight engines which were delivered to the Western Region in the summer of 1951 were shedded at Old Oak Common, Laira and Newton Abbot and were not well received at first by crews. This was hardly surprising as they were replacing their beloved GWR Castles, but after they were all eventually transferred to Cardiff Canton, they performed well on South Wales expresses. No. 70026 *Polar Star* was one of the second batch of five engines for the Western Region, Nos. 70025—29, all of which were first allocated to Cardiff Canton. These all had type BR1A tenders with an increased water capacity of 5000 gallons but the same coal capacity as the type BR1 tenders. It is seen shortly after leaving Cardiff on the up 'Red Dragon' on 30th May, 1953.   *S. Rickard*

Plate 11: Right
With ornate headboard and Cardiff Canton shedplate, No. 70024 *Vulcan* prepares to leave Paddington on the 17.55 South Wales departure, the 'Red Dragon'. The first 25 engines, Nos. 70000—70024, together with Nos. 70030—70044 all had type BR1 tenders with a capacity of 4250 gallons of water and seven tons of coal.

M. Welch

SOUTH WALES EXPRESSES

Plate 12: Above
An evening scene inside Paddington on 6th November, 1952. No. 70020 *Mercury* was one of the first eight engines delivered to the Western Region in 1951 and is awaiting departure at the head of the 18.55 for Swansea.

B. Morrison

Plate 13: Right
After No. 70026 *Polar Star* was involved in a serious derailment near Didcot in 1955 whilst working an up South Wales excursion, (see Plates 24 and 25) the handrails were removed from the smoke deflectors of some of the Western Region Britannias in order to improve forward vision from the footplate. Six hand holds were then cut into the deflectors of some of these locomotives, with brass edging, as seen here on No. 70023 *Venus* passing West Ealing on the down 'Capitals United Express' on 16th June, 1956. *R.E. Vincent*

Plate 14: *Above*   No. 70020 *Mercury* is fitted with modified grab rails and hand holds on the deflector plates and is
passing through Sonning Cutting on a down South Wales
express on 14th June, 1959.   *Peter Groom*

Plate 15: *Below*   No. 70018 *Flying Dutchman* is entering
Reading on the up 'Capitals United Express' about 1956.
                                          W. Philip Conolly

THE BOURNEMOUTH BELLE

Plate 16: Right
Nos. 70009/14 were sent on loan to the Southern shortly after delivery and they were joined by No. 70004 after the Festival of Britain Exhibition of 1951 had ended. Nos. 70004/14 were allocated to Stewarts Lane depot for use on boat trains to Dover, but for the short period whilst No. 70009 *Alfred the Great* was on the Southern, it was allocated to Nine Elms and was used on the 'Bournemouth Belle'. It is receiving last minute attention from driver A. Lay at Waterloo before departure on the down train.
C.R.L. Coles

Plate 17: Below
On 23rd June, 1951 it is passing Clapham Junction on the down train. The SR lamp brackets fitted inside the smoke deflectors can be seen in these two pictures.
B. Morrison

ON THE SOUTHERN

Plate 18: Above The two Stewarts Lane Britannias remained on the Southern until 1958 and No. 70014 *Iron Duke* is climbing Hildenborough Bank on 3rd August, 1951, when only a few weeks old, heading an up boat train.

R.E. Vincent

Plate 19: Left In 1953 the SR Merchant Navy Pacifics were withdrawn from service for examination of the driving axles, and as a result ten of the Britannias then allocated to the Western Region were loaned to the Southern. No. 70029 *Shooting Star* is leaving Salisbury on 10th August, 1953 with a special for Waterloo.

W. Philip Conolly

Plate 20: Below Again on 10th August, 1953 an up express is seen leaving Salisbury, this time behind No. 70028 *Royal Star*.

W. Philip Conolly

ON THE MANCHESTER TRAINS

Plate 21: *Above*   Three Britannias, Nos. 70034/43/44 were allocated to Longsight after delivery for use on expresses from Manchester London Road to Euston, with several more finding their way there by the early 1960s. Britannias were also used on London expresses from Manchester Central to St. Pancras via the Midland route through the Peak District, and several were shedded at Trafford Park. No. 70014 *Iron Duke* is seen on a Midland route up Manchester express in Edwalton cutting, soon after leaving Nottingham in April 1959, not long after leaving the Southern and certainly not in the fine condition in which it was kept at Stewarts Lane.   *J.P. Wilson*

Plate 22: *Above*
Nos. 70043/44 were delivered new in June 1953 with dual braking. The Westinghouse air brake compressors seen here at the front of the engine prevented the fitting of smoke deflectors and these two engines were used on trials with mineral trains on the Midland main line as well as on normal express passenger duties. No. 70043 was named *Lord Kitchener* when the air brake equipment was later removed and smoke deflectors fitted. It is seen on an up Manchester express passing Tring cutting South box.
                W. Philip Conolly

Plate 23: *Right*
No. 70044 was named *Earl Haig* when deflectors were fitted, and it is standing inside Euston in 1959 after arrival with the 'Mancunian'.
                M. Welch

Plates 24 and 25: On 20th November, 1955 one of the Cardiff Canton Britannias, No. 70026 *Polar Star*, was involved in a serious accident at Milton, between Steventon and Didcot, whilst heading an up excursion train from South Wales. Eleven people were killed and about 150 injured when the train was derailed, and later when an enquiry was held it was suggested that the driver's forward vision from the cab had been impaired. As a result, in an effort to improve forward vision from the footplate, the smoke deflectors on some of the Britannias then allocated to the Western Region were modified as described in Plates 13 and 14.

British Rail/OPC

Plate 26: Above Not surprisingly No. 70004 *William Shakespeare* is admired at Victoria just before departure on the down train on 21st April, 1956.

C.R.L. Coles

Plate 29: Above
In 1956 No. 70004 *William Shakespeare* makes a fine sight in Folkestone Warren at the head of the up train from Dover.

    A. Cawston, D. Cobbe collection

Plate 30: Left
The down 'Golden Arrow' speeds towards Ashford, near Pluckley, about 1954 behind No. 70014 *Iron Duke.*

    J. Stredwick

UNDER THE WIRES

Plate 31: Above The Britannias achieved their most resounding successes working rejuvenated trains on the Great Eastern Line of the Eastern Region after an enthusiastic welcome from crews who had previously had nothing more powerful than Class 4 and 5 power in the shape of B1s, B12s and B17s. In July 1951, No. 70002 *Geoffrey Chaucer* heads a down continental express past Stratford.   *C.R.L. Coles*

Plate 32: Below
No. 70036 *Boadicea* was one of twenty-three Britannias initially allocated to the Great Eastern line and on 30th June, 1954 it is heading a Cromer and Sheringham—Liverpool Street express near Shenfield.   *B. Morrison*

Plate 33: Above Nos. 70030–33 were allocated to Holyhead when new late in 1952 for the North Wales services to Euston, but they were found to have insufficient coal capacity for the long run to Euston. They were followed by five further engines in the summer of 1953, Nos. 70045–49, which were the first five of the final batch of ten engines, all of which were fitted with type BRID tenders which had a capacity of 4725 gallons of water and an increased capacity of 9 tons of coal. These BRID tenders were straight-sided with a curved top, had steam-operated coal pushers and weighed 54.5 tons when full, compared to the 47 tons 4 cwt of the BRI tender. No. 70045 *Lord Rowallan* is leaving Chester General on 30th May, 1964 with the 08.10 S.O. Holyhead–Crewe.

J.S. Whiteley

CHESTER FOR NORTH WALES

Plate 34: *Bottom Left*
No. 70048, later named *The Territorial Army 1908–1958*, is seen in the mid 1950s near Colwyn Bay heading the up 'Irish Mail'.
N. Stead

Plate 35: *Right*
No. 70033 *Charles Dickens* nears Saltney Junction, shortly after leaving Chester, heading the 11.55 Manchester Exchange—Llandudno and Holyhead on 7th August, 1961.
J.S. Whiteley

Plate 36: *Left*   On the North Wales coast at Aber, between Bangor and Llandudno Junction, No. 70047 is at the head of the up 'Irish Mail' on 9th July, 1959. No. 70047 was unique in being the only Britannia, for some unknown reason, never to have received a name. The names conferred on the Britannias were varied to say the least, ranging from famous British writers, poets, military celebrities, Scottish Firths, past Great Western names, historical figures and others. Inspiration, however, appears to have deserted the authorities so far as 70047 was concerned.
British Rail/OPC

Plate 37: *Below*   On 31st March, 1963 No. 70019 *Lightning* displays a fine exhaust passing West Shore, near Deganwy heading an afternoon Llandudno—Birmingham train.
G.W. Morrison

Plate 38: *Above* An interesting picture of No. 70009 *Alfred the Great* taken at Llandudno Junction on 13th May, 1951 heading a Llandudno—Birmingham New Street train. The engine is brand new from Crewe works and on one of its first outings. It is not carrying a shed code, was officially allocated to Norwich but in fact was sent almost immediately on loan to the Southern Region.   *J.P. Wilson*

Plate 39: *Below* In the picturesque setting of Conway Castle on 28th August, 1964, No. 70050 *Firth of Clyde* is heading a relief to the up 'Irish Mail'. The BR AWS battery box can be seen on the running plate in front of the firebox.
D. Cross

Plate 40: *Above*   The last five Britannias delivered late in the summer of 1954, Nos. 70050–54, were allocated to Scotland and were shedded at Polmadie. They were named after Scottish Firths and were mainly used on Manchester and Liverpool expresses. Gradually, however, during the mid 1960s, the majority of the class were moved to Carlisle Kingmoor and were used on the West Coast main line, to Manchester, Liverpool, Perth and over the Settle and Carlisle. No. 70035 *Rudyard Kipling* is climbing towards Dunblane on 24th August, 1964 heading the 09.25 Crewe–Perth and Aberdeen.

J.S. Whiteley

Plate 41: *Below* Unlike most other express passenger locomotives, some of the Britannias ran for a few years bereft of name-plates which were removed for safe keeping. No. 70031 (*Byron*) has also lost its shed plate and has had the top lamp bracket lowered to the centre left of the smokebox door. It is standing inside Perth on an up fish train on 8th June, 1965.

J.S. Whiteley

Plate 42: *Left* No. 70047 of Crewe North nears the border at Kirkpatrick heading a Glasgow—Birmingham express on 4th June, 1960.

G.W. Morrison

Plate 43: *Below* Early on the morning of 21st April, 1965, No. 70005 (*John Milton*) leaves Stirling on a short parcels for Perth.

J.S. Whiteley

Plate 44: *Above*   On 18th February, 1961 No. 70044 *Earl Haig* streaks along near Lamington heading an early morning Carlisle–Glasgow Central. This was the last Britannia to be built with a type BR1 tender.   *D. Cross*

Plate 45: *Below*   No. 70035 *Rudyard Kipling* was one of five Britannias, Nos. 70035–39, which were built with roller bearings on only the driving wheels. It is seen leaving Dunblane on an up parcels train on 11th August, 1964.

D. Cross

Plate 46: Above Awaiting departure at Liverpool Street for Norwich on the early evening of the 11th March, 1952 is Stratford Britannia No. 70002 *Geoffrey Chaucer.*

B. Morrison

Plate 47: Above   On the 23rd April, 1954 No. 70001 *Lord Hurcomb* passes Trowse cattle dock heading the up 'East Anglian'.   *R.E. Vincent*

Plate 48: Below   The up train is seen again, this time on 2nd September, 1955 shortly after leaving Norwich Thorpe behind No. 70005 *John Milton*.   *Peter Groom*

Plate 49: *Above* Generally speaking, WR crews did not get on well with the Britannias, the exception being footplatemen at Cardiff Canton who produced some fine performances. On 22nd April, 1954 No. 70026 *Polar Star* passes Rumney River Bridge box heading a Swansea—Manchester express. *S. Rickard*

EASTBOUND FROM CARDIFF

Plate 50: *Below* Early in 1953 No. 70025 *Western Star*, another one of the five Cardiff Canton Britannias with BRIA tender, is passing Pengam Sidings on a Swansea—Manchester express. *S. Rickard*

NEAR THE SEVERN TUNNEL

Plate 51: Above An interesting scene at Severn Tunnel Junction on 21st May, 1958 as No. 70025 *Western Star* eases a West to North express through the station. *S. Rickard*

Plate 52: Below The down 'South Wales Pullman' speeds over Magor Watertroughs, just West of Severn Tunnel Junction, behind No. 70018 *Flying Dutchman* on 26th June, 1956. *S. Rickard*

Plate 53: *Above*   Whilst allocated to Old Oak Common, No. 70017 *Arrow* accelerates a Paddington express along the sea wall at Teignmouth.   *J.K. Morton*

Plate 54: *Above Right*   Some of the Western Region engines found their way into Cornwall and No. 70016 *Ariel* ▷ of Laira is seen between Lostwithiel and Bodmin Road heading the up 'Cornishman', the 10.35 Penzance—Wolverhampton. 25th June, 1955.   *R.E. Vincent*

Plate 55: *Bottom Right*   Another one of the Laira engines, No. 70021 *Morning Star* heads west into Cornwall on the ▷ down 'Cornish Riviera' seen passing Saltash on 14th April, 1952.   *R.E. Vincent*

Plate 56: *Above Left* Northbound trains often took banking assistance from Tebay for the 5¾ miles of mainly 1 in 75 to Shap Summit. No. 70032 (*Tennyson*) nears Shap Wells with banking assistance on a heavy down freight on 1st April, 1967. *J.S. Whiteley*

Plate 57: *Below Left* The driver of No. 70038 *Robin Hood* almost has the summit in sight whilst heading a Manchester–Glasgow express on 4th July, 1964. *G.W. Morrison*

Plate 58: *Above* The fireman is taking a welcome breather in this picture of No. 70042 *Lord Roberts* heading the Sunday down 'Mid-Day Scot' on 26th July, 1964.

J.S. Whiteley

Plate 59: *Above*   No. 70032 (*Tennyson*) is climbing past Greenholme towards Scout Green on a northbound freight.
M. Welch

Plate 60: *Below*   Double-headed Pacifics was a rare sight, but on 31st July, 1965 Nos. 70013 (*Oliver Cromwell*) and 70039 (*Sir Christopher Wren*) combine efforts heading a 15 coach Bank Holiday relief to the down 'Mid-Day Scot', seen nearing Scout Green.
M. Welch

Plate 61: *Above* On 25th August, 1961 No. 70045 *Lord Rowallan* restarts from Tebay after taking banking assistance whilst heading a Manchester—Glasgow express.

D. Cross

Plate 62: *Right* No. 70052 (*Firth of Tay*) is going extremely well past Greenholme heading a down relief on 30th July, 1965.　M. Welch

GREAT NORTHERN FROM KINGS CROSS

Plate 63: Above Several Britannias were transferred to Immingham depot after the Great Eastern line was dieselised, and amongst their duties were workings to Kings Cross. On 17th August, 1961 No. 70040 *Clive of India* roars out of Hadley North Tunnel heading a Kings Cross—Cleethorpes express. *D. Cross*

Plate 64: Below Another Immingham engine, No. 70039 *Sir Christopher Wren*, is seen emerging from Wood Green Tunnel on the 16.10 Kings Cross—Grimsby and Cleethorpes express on 15th June, 1962. *Peter Groom*

CARLISLE DEPARTURES

Plate 65: Right
No. 70035 (*Rudyard Kipling*) makes a vigorous departure from Carlisle past Number 4 box on 14th April, 1965 heading a down relief.

D. Cross

Plate 66: Below
The City of Carlisle can be seen in the background in this picture of No. 70003 *John Bunyan* crossing the River Eden near Kingmoor Depot heading a Glasgow parcels. 6th September, 1964.

D. Cross

ON SHED AT WILLESDEN

Plate 67: Above On 26th June, 1964 No. 70014 *Iron Duke* has an assortment of companions whilst waiting its next turn of duty.

Peter Groom

Plate 68: Below The graceful lines of No. 70042 *Lord Roberts* can be seen in this side view, together with the footblock which was added to the tenders to aid watering.

Peter Groom

ON SHED AT HOLBECK

Plate 69: Right
No. 70050 *Firth of Clyde* has just had its tender replenished underneath the coaler on 1st July, 1962. A diesel hauled express to St. Pancras can be seen in the background.   *J.S. Whitley*

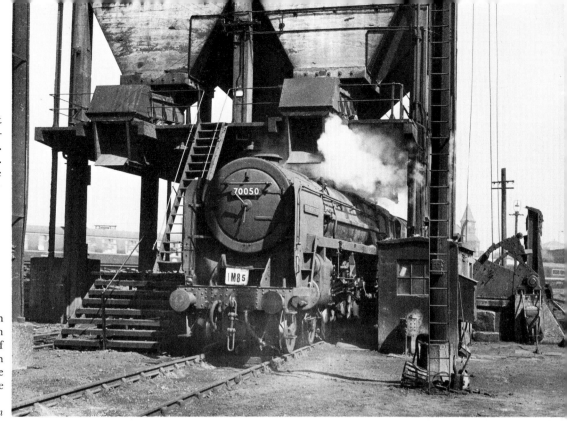

Plate 70: Below
No. 70021 (*Morning Star*) is seen from inside the roundhouse on 6th September, 1967, in its last year of service. This was one of the Western Region engines which did not have the handrails removed from the smoke deflectors.

G.W. Morrison

LIVERPOOL STREET DEPARTURES

Plate 71: Above A majestic start by No. 70003 *John Bunyan* on 15th August, 1951 whilst heading the down 'Norfolkman'.   *R.E. Vincent*

Plate 72: Below The customary murk of Liverpool Street can be seen in this picture of No. 70010 *Owen Glendower* leaving on 3rd September, 1951 heading a Yarmouth train.   *J.P. Wilson*

DEPARTURES FROM NORWICH

Plate 73: Left
By April 1961, diesels had started to appear on the Great Eastern as can be seen in this picture of No. 70013 *Oliver Cromwell* leaving on an express for Liverpool Street.

J.S. Whiteley

Plate 74: Below
On 10th April, 1961 No. 70006 *Robert Burns* is negotiating the Wensum triangle shortly after leaving Norwich Thorpe on an express for Liverpool Street.

Peter Groom

Plate 75: Above No. 70022 *Tornado* runs alongside the sea wall at Teignmouth heading the northbound 'Devonian'.
J.K. Morton

Plate 76: Above Right On 27th June, 1955 No. 70016 *Ariel* is about to enter Mutley Tunnel shortly after leaving ▷ Plymouth North Road with the 9 coach 14.00 to Paddington.
R.E. Vincent

Plate 77: Bottom Right No. 70027 *Rising Star* picks up water from Goring troughs in September 1959 whilst head- ▷ ing an express from Swansea to Paddington.

D. Cross

Plate 78: *Above*   Under a beautiful sky No. 70018 *Flying Dutchman* nears Exminster at the head of a late afternoon passenger and mail from Plymouth.

J. Stredwick

Plate 79: *Below*   Sonning Cutting provides an attractive setting for No. 70029 *Shooting Star* heading an express from Paddington to Swansea on 16th August, 1961.

D. Cross

Plate 80: Above On the North and West route at Craven Arms, No. 70025 *Western Star* is heading a pigeon special from Heysham to Weymouth on 5th June, 1964.

D. Cross

CROSS COUNTRY

Plate 81: Below No. 70001 *Lord Hurcomb* approaches Cheltenham Lansdown on 9th June, 1964 heading a Bristol—Birmingham train. The lines on the left hand side of the picture form the Great Western to Swindon.

D. Cross

DILLICAR TROUGHS, TEBAY

Plate 82: Above No. 70015 *Apollo* speeds south and replenishes its tender heading the 11.50 Glasgow—Morecambe train on 27th June, 1964.

J.S. Whiteley

Plate 83: Below The troughs ran parallel with the River Lune and No. 70044 *Earl Haig* picks up water on the morning Glasgow—Birmingham express on 12th April, 1963, between intermittent snow showers.

J.S. Whiteley

Plate 84: *Above* Again on the 12th April, 1963 No. 70017 *Arrow* accelerates over the troughs towards Tebay and takes a run at the climb to Shap Summit.

J.S. Whiteley

Plate 85: *Below* Not ideal weather for photography on 9th December, 1967 but the conditions have provided an interesting photograph of No. 70023 *Venus* heading a northbound freight.

G.W. Morrison

Plate 86: Above The down 'Waverley' is seen on 5th March, 1960 near Horton-in-Ribblesdale behind Holbeck Britannia No. 70053 *Moray Firth*.

G.W. Morrison

Plate 87: Below A southbound freight is passing No. 70029 (*Shooting Star*) at Stainforth whilst heading a down freight. It has steam to spare but still a long way to go to the summit at Blea Moor. 18th April, 1967.

G.W. Morrison

Plate 88: *Above*   The same train is seen again, at Ribblehead, nearing the end of the 'long drag'.

G.W. Morrison

Plate 89: *Below*   A feature of the climb from Settle Junction to Blea Moor is the 440 yd long Batty Moss Viaduct at Ribblehead and No. 70054 *Dornoch Firth* is crossing on 16th May, 1959 heading the down 'Thames—Clyde Express'.

G.W. Morrison

Plate 90: *Above* On a fine summer's day No. 70051 *Firth of Forth* comes out of the cutting at the approach to Shap Summit from the south, heading an afternoon Manchester—Glasgow express. 24th August, 1962.

G.W. Morrison

Plate 91: *Below* Unnamed No. 70047 is seen near Frizinghall in July 1967 heading an evening freight from Bradford, Valley Road Goods, to Carlisle.

J.S. Whiteley

BOAT TRAINS

Plate 92: Left
Whilst at Stewarts Lane, No. 70014 *Iron Duke* was seen on continental expresses between Victoria and Dover. On 23rd May, 1953 it is racing down Hildenborough Bank heading a down express.

B. Morrison

Plate 93: Below
Iron Duke is seen again, leaving Sandling Tunnel in 1952 heading a down boat train.

A Cawston, D. Cobbe collection

Plate 94: *Above* Apart from Shap, the other notorious climb on the West Coast main line was from Beattock Station to the summit at 1015 ft above sea level, almost exactly half way between Carlisle and Glasgow. No. 70046 *Anzac* is passing Harthope with banking assistance heading the 09.30 Manchester—Glasgow on 21st April, 1962.

J.S. Whiteley

BEATTOCK BANK

Plate 95: *Below* On the early morning of 23rd April, 1962 No. 70022 *Tornado* goes effortlessly up the gradient near Greskine heading the 07.12 Lockerbie—Glasgow stopping train.

J.S. Whiteley

Plate 96: *Above* On 15th April, 1963 No. 70019 *Lightning* is passing Harthope heading the 09.43 Liverpool— Edinburgh and Glasgow. Banking assistance had been taken at Beattock Station for the 10 mile climb to the summit.

J.S. Whiteley

Plate 97: *Below* The 09.30 Manchester—Glasgow is seen behind No. 70037 *Hereward the Wake* still carrying an Immingham shed plate but shortly after being transferred to Carlisle Kingmoor. 15th April, 1963.

J.S. Whiteley

THE WAVERLEY

Plate 98: *Above* The 09.15 St. Pancras–Edinburgh Waverley was given the title of 'The Waverley' and the down train is seen leaving Leeds City on 8th March, 1961 behind No. 70044 *Earl Haig.*   *G.W. Morrison*

Plate 99: *Below* With steam to spare, No. 70054 *Dornoch Firth* passes Whitehall Junction shortly after leaving Leeds City, again on the down train.   *G.W. Morrison*

Plate 100: Right
Clan Pacific No. 72006 *Clan Mackenzie* rests between duties at Leeds Holbeck on 21st August, 1961.

G.W. Morrison

Plate 101: Below
On an attractive rake of all maroon coaches, Clan No. 72008 *Clan Macleod* passes Morecambe South Junction with a Manchester—Glasgow express on 29th August, 1964.

G.W. Morrison

Plate 102: Right
Clan No. 72007 *Clan Mackintosh* is seen with a full head of steam on freight duty, passing Wortley Junction, shortly after leaving Leeds, with an afternoon train for Carlisle. 10th September, 1963.

G.W. Morrison

Plate 103: *Above*
The 15.25 Stourton (Leeds)—Carlisle became a frequent Britannia working between 1965 and 1967. Here we see No. 70029 (*Shooting Star*) heading the train north away from Skipton on 18th April, 1967.
G.W. Morrison

EXITS FROM SKIPTON

Plate 104: *Right*
At the south end of Skipton No. 70003 (*John Bunyan*) is about to pass under the former Ilkley line as it heads an up express freight from Carlisle on 8th March, 1967.
G.W. Morrison

SHAP WELLS

Plate 105: *Right*
On a dull and blustery day No. 70002 *Geoffrey Chaucer* passes Shap Wells on the climb from Tebay to Shap Summit heading the 14.00 Manchester—Glasgow. 27th June, 1964.

J.S. Whiteley

Plate 106: *Below*
No. 70041 (*Sir John Moore*) has steam to spare with 13 coaches behind the tender, as it blasts its way past Shap Wells towards the summit, which is only about another mile. 17th July, 1965.

J.S. Whiteley

Plate 107: *Top*   Once the pride of Stewarts Lane, No. 70004 (*William Shakespeare*) is leaving Valley Road Goods, Bradford on 19th June, 1967 on the 19.40 freight to Carlisle.

J.S. Whiteley

Plate 108: *Centre*   No. 70038 (*Robin Hood*) arrives at Bradford, Forster Square on an afternoon parcels from Leeds on 15th March, 1967.

J.S. Whiteley

Plate 109: *Left*   The same parcels train is seen on 11th March, 1967 passing the box at Shipley Bradford Junction behind No. 70027 (*Rising Star*).

J.S. Whiteley

LEEDS DEPARTURES

Plate 110: Left
No. 70008 *Black Prince* passes under the Great Northern line into Leeds Central whilst heading the 16.55 Leeds City—Morecambe express at Holbeck Low Level on 13th July, 1964.

G.W. Morrison

Plate 111: Below
No. 70044 *Earl Haig* was one of the three Britannias, Nos. 70044/53/54, which replaced some rebuilt Scots at Holbeck depot around 1959. It is passing Wortley Junction soon after leaving Leeds City, on the down 'Waverley' express. 9th March, 1961.

G.W. Morrison

Plate 112: *Above*   There is no mistaking this train as anything other than a football special, as some young supporters from Barrow hurl toilet rolls from the window as the train passes through Marsh Lane cutting, Leeds on its way to Hull, behind No. 70025 (*Western Star*). The locomotive worked right through to Hull, which must have been one of the very few occasions on which a Britannia visited the city. 18th March, 1967.   *G.W. Morrison*

Plate 113: *Below*   The fireman takes a well earned rest after shovelling most of the way from Carlisle to Ais Gill Summit on No. 70010 *Owen Glendower*. The train is a return special carrying Welsh rugby fans back to Cardiff from Edinburgh, and is seen here approaching Shotlock Hill Tunnel on 5th February, 1967.

G.W. Morrison

Plate 114: *Above* No. 70010 *Owen Glendower* disturbs the peace of a Sunday morning, as it blasts its way through Kirkby Stephen towards Ais Gill Summit on the same train as seen in the previous picture.

G.W. *Morrison*

Plate 115: *Below* The clouds hang low on Wild Boar Fell as No. 70039 (*Sir Christopher Wren*) passes Ais Gill Summit on another special conveying Welsh rugby supporters back to Cardiff on 5th February, 1967.

G.W. *Morrison*

Plate 116: Above A brief gap in the clouds allows the sun to shine for a moment on No. 70039 (*Sir Christopher Wren*) as it passes Kirkby Stephen with one of the five returning rugby supporters specials from Edinburgh to Cardiff. 5th February, 1967. *G.W. Morrison*

Plate 117: Below High up on the side of the Mallerstang Valley, No. 70003 (*John Bunyan*) is making good progress towards Ais Gill Summit on another of the return rugby specials from Edinburgh to Wales. 5th February, 1967. *G.W. Morrison*

Plate 118: *Above*   No. 70047 catches the evening sun on 12th July, 1967 whilst approaching Shipley on the 19.40 freight from Bradford to Carlisle.

J.S. Whiteley

Plate 119: *Below*   During its extensive use on special rail tours towards the end of steam on BR, No. 70013 *Oliver Cromwell*, with its name painted on the smoke deflectors, is taking the Penistone route out of Huddersfield at Springwood Junction in October, 1967.   *J.S. Whiteley*

FREIGHT FROM BRADFORD

Plate 120: Above No. 70034 (*Thomas Hardy*) is ready to leave Valley Road goods yard on the 19.40 freight to Carlisle on 27th June, 1966.

G.W. Morrison

Plate 121: Below No. 70048 (*The Territorial Army 1908–1958*) at the head of the same freight at Valley Road in March 1967.

J.S. Whiteley

Plates 122 & 123: Two views of the 15.40 all stations to Carlisle leaving Forster Square, Bradford, *Above* behind No. 70051 (*Firth of Forth*) and *Below* No. 70001 (*Lord Hurcomb*), both taken in April, 1966.
Photos J.S. Whiteley

PASSENGER FROM BRADFORD

THE BROADSMAN

Plate 125: Below A fine view of No. 70013 *Oliver Cromwell* waiting to leave Liverpool Street on the down train on 3rd September, 1951.

J.P. Wilson

Plate 124: Above No. 70007 *Coeur-de-Lion* carrying a special headboard during the Coronation year, makes an impressive entrance into Ipswich after its 1 hour 13 minute run from Liverpool Street. 28th May, 1953.

R.E. Vincent

EAST ANGLIAN EXPRESSES

Plate 126: Above   The up 'Scandinavian' is headed by an immaculate No. 70037 *Hereward the Wake* near Shenfield on 8th May, 1955. King Frederick of Denmark was travelling in the Royal Saloon.   *R.E. Vincent*

Plate 127: Below   Over a year later and still looking as immaculate as ever No. 70037 *Hereward the Wake* storms out of Liverpool Street station with the down 'Day Continental'. 20th June, 1956.   *R.E. Vincent*

WITH ASSISTANCE

Plate 128: Above No. 70032 (*Tennyson*) is working hard up Grayrigg bank near Lambrigg Crossing, which is between Oxenholme and Tebay, on a heavy northbound freight. It is being assisted at the rear by a 2-6-4T which would have been attached at Oxenholme. 1st April, 1967.

G.W. Morrison

Plate 129: Below Class 2P 4-4-0 No. 40694 of Preston was doing little to assist No. 70054 *Dornoch Firth* haul this massive 17 coach Manchester–Glasgow express up Shap on 26th May, 1958. The pair are seen just before entering the summit cutting.

G.W. Morrison

SOME EVENTS OF NOTE

Plate 130: Left
No. 70037 *Hereward the Wake* along with other BR standard designs was present at the International Railway Congress Exhibition, held in Willesden roundhouse. 27th May, 1954.

R.E. Vincent

Plate 131: Below left
The naming ceremony of No. 70045 *Lord Rowallan* at Euston on 16th July, 1957 was attended by the Chief Scout, Lord Rowallan, and the Chairman of the L.M. Regional Board, Lord Rusholme. Both are seen here striding down platform 6 with stationmaster Harry Turrell.

M. Welch

Plate 132: Above
After the naming ceremony, the scouts get an opportunity to inspect the locomotive more closely.

M. Welch

Plate 133: Left
A sad sight for steam enthusiasts on 2nd February, 1967, as No. 70013 *Oliver Cromwell* emerges from Crewe Works erecting shop as the last steam locomotive to be overhauled by British Rail.

British Rail L.M. Region

LEEDS NOCTURNE

Plate 134: Left
No. 70051 (*Firth of Forth*) waits at Leeds City station on a Manchester—York express in November 1967.
J.S. Whiteley

Plate 135: Below No. 70023 (*Venus*) stands in torrential rain at Leeds City, having just arrived on a Manchester—York express. Enthusiasts who had probably travelled on this, the only regular steam passenger working over the Pennines by this date, brave the elements to have a word with the crew. 27th October, 1967. *J.S. Whiteley*

IN CLOSE UP

Plate 136: *Above*
No. 70012 (*John of Gaunt*) is being inspected closely at Lancaster Castle before leaving for the north on 9th October, 1965.

G.W. Morrison

Plate 137: *Above Right*
Looking down on a Britannia at Willesden Shed with the detail of the type BRIA tender evident.

M. Welch

Plate 138: *Right*
No. 70013 *Oliver Cromwell* seen in close up at Newton Heath Shed, Manchester in 1968.

M. Welch

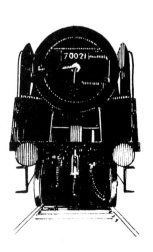

Plate 139: Above Light work for No. 70009 (*Alfred the Great*) which is nevertheless giving an impressive exhaust, as it heads an Ayr to Carlisle mail train near Garrochburn Sidings, south of Kilmarnock. 29th April, 1964.

D. Cross

Plate 140: Below No. 70039 (*Sir Christopher Wren*) passes through Blackfaulds Cutting on the approach to Polquhap Summit in the Nith Valley, between Cumnock and New Cumnock. 26th May, 1964. *D. Cross*

Plate 141: *Above* No. 70007 *Coeur-de-Lion* rolls past BR Standard class 2-6-0 No. 76097 at Falkland Junction, near Ayr, with coal empties from Glasgow.

D. Cross

Plate 142: *Below* No. 70009 (*Alfred the Great*) makes an early morning departure from Dumfries on the Carlisle—Glasgow postal and parcels train on 11th June, 1965.

M. Welch

Plate 143: *Above*　No. 70039 (*Sir Christopher Wren*) is seen passing Mauchline on a relief train to the 'Thames—Clyde Express'. The external state of the locomotive was typical of Carlisle Kingmoor Britannias during their allocation to that depot. 26th May, 1964.

D. Cross

Plate 144: *Below*　This shot of No. 70003 (*John Bunyan*) is dominated by the impressive signal gantries at Kilmarnock, as it arrives with steam to spare on a relief express from Glasgow to Leeds on 2nd August, 1966.

D. Cross

THE 12.55 HUNSLET–CARLISLE FREIGHT

Plate 145: Above   No. 70004 (*William Shakespeare*) near Calverley and Rodley on 21st August, 1967.

G.W. Morrison

Plate 146: Below   No. 70010 (*Owen Glendower*) enters Newlay cutting near Leeds on 6th July, 1967.

G.W. Morrison

NORTH LONDON

Plate 147: Above On the dull afternoon of 29th August, 1963, No. 70010 *Owen Glendower* pulls out of Camden Goods Yard on the 14.18 freight for the north.

Peter Groom

Plate 148: Below No. 70033 *Charles Dickens* working hard up Camden Bank on a Euston—Manchester express. Six Britannias including No. 70033 were allocated to Longsight at this time for working the Manchester—Euston expresses. 7th October, 1958.

B. Morrison

ON RAIL TOUR DUTY

Plate 149: Above No. 70038 *Robin Hood* with its name painted on the smoke deflector, is storming up the bank out of Huddersfield towards Standedge, near Longwood, on a SLS special returning from York. 2nd July, 1967.

G.W. Morrison

Plate 150: Below No. 70035 (*Rudyard Kipling*) approaches Ais Gill Summit whilst deputising for Jubilee Class 4-6-0 No. 45593 *Kolhapur*, which had failed at Carlisle after working the special from Bradford Forster Square on 30th April, 1966.

J.S. Whiteley

Plate 151: Above
A most unusual combination in the shape of BR standard class 4 4-6-0 and Britannia No. 70009 *Alfred the Great* seen climbing out of Leeds over the arches above Holbeck depot. The load was about 22 vans which made it hard work for the locomotives on the climb from Leeds to the summit at Morley. 11th April, 1964.

J.S. Whiteley

Plate 152: Left
The Heaton—Red Bank empty van train was normally heavily loaded being the return of vans which had worked from Manchester to Newcastle overnight with news-papers. It was one of the very few workings where you would be likely to see a Britannia and B1 together in the mid 1960s. Here we see No. 70018 (*Flying Dutchman*) and B1 No. 61030 (*Nyala*) approaching Brighouse on 28th May, 1966.

G.W. Morrison

Plate 153: *Above*   No. 70015 *Apollo* assists Stanier class 5
4-6-0 No. 45200 away from the sidings at Neville Hill, Leeds,
after changing crews. 3rd July, 1966.

G.W. Morrison

Plate 154: *Below*   On 7th May, 1966 No. 70011 (*Hotspur*)
and Black 5 No. 44947 are heading the train past Cooper
Bridge, between Mirfield and Brighouse. The lines on the
right have now been lifted, done when the junction at
Heaton Lodge was redesigned.

G.W. Morrison

AWAITING DUTY

Plate 155: Above
No. 70030 *William Wordsworth* simmers gently in the evening sun on Carnforth Shed on 26th August, 1964.

G.W. Morrison

Plate 156: Left
Holbeck depot, Leeds, is the setting for this picture of No. 70049 (*Solway Firth*) on 8th June, 1967.
G.W. Morrison

Plate 157: *Above* Perth shed nearly always allocated a Pacific for the 16.47 express fish for the south. No. 70005 (*John Milton*) carries out the duty on 21st April, 1965, in place of what had normally been a Stanier Pacific working during the earlier part of the 1960s. The train is seen leaving Stirling. *J.S. Whiteley*

Plate 158: *Below* Another view of the same train, with a cleaner Britannia, No. 70031 (*Byron*) leaving Perth on 8th June, 1965. *J.S. Whiteley*

FISH TRAFFIC

IN TROUBLE

Plates 159, 160, 161:
This sequence shows an unidentified Britannia, clearly in terrible condition, struggling up the long climb from Settle Junction to Blea Moor in its last few weeks before withdrawal. 4th November, 1967.
J.S. Whiteley

Left: Helwith Bridge.

Right: Selside.

Left: Batty Moss Viaduct, Ribblehead.

OVERTAKING FREIGHT

Plate 162: Above The driver of No. 70048 (*The Territorial Army 1908–1958*) looks back to Class 5 No. 44899 in the loop at Winwick Junction, as he heads north in grand style on a relief Euston–Glasgow Express on 23rd March, 1967.
M. Welch

Plate 163: Below No. 70028 (*Royal Star*) in very poor external condition, but with steam to spare, passes two class 8F 2-8-0s waiting in the down loop on a permanent way train, as it drifts into Oxenholme. The locomotive depot can be seen on the right of the picture. 6th August, 1966.
G.W. Morrison

BEFORE AND AFTER DEPARTURE

Plate 164: *Above*   The station clock at Carlisle shows 20.25 on the evening of 10th August, 1964, as No. 70035 *Rudyard Kipling* prepares to leave with the 13.30 Euston—Perth express.   *J.S. Whiteley*

Plate 165: *Below* An impressive signal gantry and equally impressive combination of motive power at Shrewsbury on 13th June, 1953, showing No. 70043, later named *Lord Kitchener*, waiting to leave on the 12.15 stopper to Crewe, and Stanier Pacific No. 46245 *City of London* taking water in the centre road.   *L.N. Owen*

Plate 166: Above Unusual motive power for the Calder Valley main line in the early 1960s was No. 70036 *Boadicea*, seen passing Sowerby Bridge on a Scunthorpe–Blackpool excursion. The locomotive was shedded at Immingham at that time. 8th September, 1963. *J.K. Morton*

Plate 167: Below No. 70000 *Britannia* itself, a long way from its home depot of Stratford, pulls out of Sheffield Victoria, having taken over from an electric locomotive on the Liverpool–Parkeston Quay boat train on 20th September, 1958. In 1958 this was a new Stratford diagram for the Britannia Pacifics. The engine worked to Parkeston on an evening freight, then to Sheffield and back, returning to Stratford on another evening freight. Crews were changed at Parkeston, Ipswich and March in each direction. *J.K. Morton*

FREIGHT AND PARCELS TRAFFIC

Plate 168: Left
No. 70032 (*Tennyson*) hurries through the Lune Valley on a down freight, trying to keep out of the way of preserved A4 No. 4498 *Sir Nigel Gresley* which was not very far behind on its first outing after restoration heading a Crewe—Carlisle special. 1st April, 1967.
G.W. Morrison

Plate 169: Below
No. 70036 (*Boadicea*) trundles past Carlisle Kingmoor locomotive depot on a freight whilst heading for the marshalling yard. 23rd April, 1966.
G.W. Morrison

Plate 170: Right
The 15.17 Bradford Forster Square —Heysham parcels near Gargrave headed by No. 70025 (*Western Star*) on a dull, misty day. 16th September, 1967.

J.S. Whiteley

Plate 171: Left
No. 70032 (*Tennyson*) rounds the sharp curve off the Bradford line at Shipley, Bingley Junction on the evening 19.40 Valley Road Goods— Carlisle freight. 13th July, 1967.

J.S. Whiteley

Plate 172: Right
No. 70024 (*Vulcan*) makes an impressive exhaust whilst tackling the climb from Carlisle to Shap Summit. It is seen just before entering the cutting near Shap Station on 4th November, 1967.

J.S. Whiteley

Plate 173: *Above* One of the last steam workings from Carlisle Kingmoor depot was the 08.05 Carlisle—Red Bank van train, which is seen near Appleby behind No. 70045 *Lord Rowallan*, diverted on this occasion via Ais Gill due to a derailment near Penrith. Note the oval buffers attached to the locomotive at this time. December, 1967.　　　　*J.S. Whiteley*

BETWEEN APPLEBY
AND AIS GILL

Plate 174: *Right*
No. 70002 *Geoffrey Chaucer* leaves Birkett Tunnel on an up relief to the 'Waverley' express. 4th July, 1964.　　　*G.W. Morrison*

Plate 175: Above On one of its many railtour activities towards the end of steam on BR, No. 70013 heads a special, near Buxworth, commemorating the centenary of the completion of the Midland main line into St. Pancras. 9th June, 1968.

J.S. Whiteley

OLIVER CROMWELL ON TOUR

Plate 176: *Above*   On 16th June, 1968 No. 70013 made a trip from Todmorden to Preston, Carnforth and back to Skipton for the West Riding Branch of the R.C.T.S. It is seen just south of Hellifield on the return.

J.S. Whiteley

Plate 177: *Below*   On 28th October, 1967 it is seen bursting out of Elland Tunnel on the Calder Valley main line, on an outing from Manchester to Huddersfield, Penistone and Sheffield.   *G.W. Morrison*

Plate 178: Above With only two weeks remaining for steam on BR, No. 70013 performs on a special organised by the Manchester Rail Travel Society, the 'Farewell to BR Steam' railtour. It is leaving the tunnel at Gisburn on its way from Blackburn to Skipton. 28th July, 1968. *J.S. Whiteley*

Plate 179: Below Sunday 11th August, 1968 was a sad day for all steam enthusiasts in Britain, as it marked the end of steam on British Rail. 1T57 was organised by BR as the last steam hauled railtour which ran from Liverpool Lime Street to Carlisle and back with tickets costing 15 guineas per head. *Oliver Cromwell* had the honour of sharing part of the working of this train, between Manchester Victoria and Carlisle via Blackburn. It is seen crossing Batty Moss Viaduct at Ribblehead, a spectacle witnessed by many hundreds of people. Thankfully, however, this was not to be the last time steam appeared on BR due to the efforts of many individuals and Railway Preservation Societies.

J.S. Whiteley

DUKE OF GLOUCESTER

Plate 180: *Above*   No. 71000 *Duke of Gloucester* was the only BR standard Class 8, and had it not been for the Harrow and Wealdstone disaster in October 1952 in which LMR Pacific No. 46202 *Princess Anne* was destroyed, it might never have been constructed. As it was, it emerged from Crewe Works early in 1954, more similar in appearance to the Britannias than the Stanier Pacifics. Unlike the Britannias, however, it incorporated three cylinders, and the piston valves were replaced by Caprotti gear and poppet valves. It had a Britannia boiler with the same 250 lb psi pressure, but the grate area was increased from 42 sq. ft. to 48.6 sq. ft. A double chimney and blastpipe was fitted, unlike the Britannias, but it retained the 6ft 2in diameter driving wheels. In 1958 it is awaiting departure from platform 13 at Euston on the 'Mid-Day Scot'.

M. Welch

Plate 181: *Right*   For its entire working life, short though it may have been, it was allocated to Crewe North shed and worked over the West Coast main line. It was often seen on the 'Mid-Day Scot' and on 5th April, 1957 it is passing Watford Junction on the down train.

British Rail/OPC

Plate 182: *Above*   A comparison of front ends at Euston with No. 71000 again on the down 'Mid-Day Scot' and 'Coronation' Pacific No. 46238 *City of Carlisle* on the 13.35 to Perth. Although 71000 put up some good performances with enthusiastic crews, it was generally thought that further study was needed before the engine could develop its full potential. As a result of the decision to switch from steam to diesel and electric traction the design was never fully investigated and the engine ran basically unaltered until withdrawal in November 1962.   *M. Welch*

Plate 183: *Below*   During its working life it did gain a reputation for being heavy on coal and this was one of the reasons why the LMR crews preferred their Stanier Pacifics, particularly the 'Coronations'. No. 71000 was fitted with a one-off tender which was classified type BR1J and which had a capacity of 10 tons of coal with a steam-operated coal pusher, and 4325 gallons of water. On 9th August, 1955 it is leaving Crewe heading a Birmingham–Manchester express.   *B. Morrison*

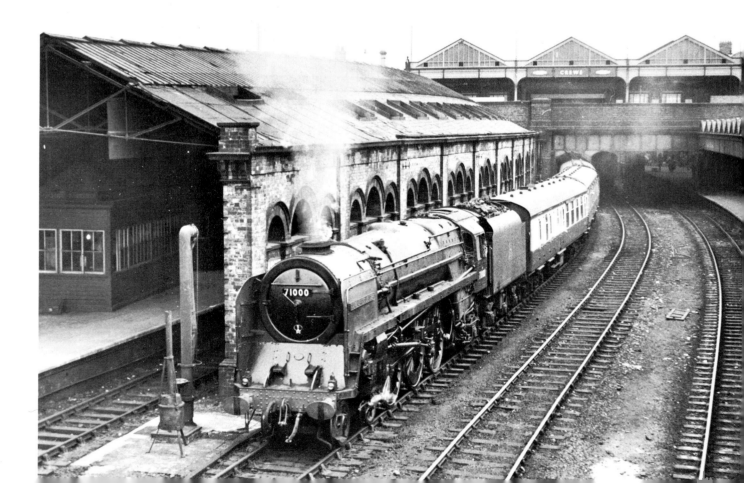

Plate 184: Above On 31st October, 1954 it is seen in Swindon Works yard during tests on the Western Region.
B. Morrison

Plate 185: Below No. 71000 is climbing Camden Bank on the down 'Mid-Day Scot' in October 1956. It was withdrawn from service in November 1962 and remained at Crewe for several years before being sent to Barry scrapyard for breaking up. It was, however, rescued in 1973 and is being restored at Loughborough on the Main Line Steam Trust.
Peter Groom

SUMMARY

BR No.	Name	Date Built	W/D
72000	Clan Buchanan	12/51	12/62
72001	Clan Cameron	12/51	12/62
72002	Clan Campbell	1/52	12/62
72003	Clan Fraser	1/52	12/62
72004	Clan Macdonald	2/52	12/62
72005	Clan Macgregor	2/52	4/65
72006	Clan Mackenzie	2/52	5/66
72007	Clan Mackintosh	2/52	12/65
72008	Clan Macleod	2/52	4/66
72009	Clan Stewart	3/52	8/65

Plate 186: Top   The pleasing lines of the Clans can be seen in this picture of No. 72005 *Clan Macgregor* taken at Perth, before it received BR AWS equipment, but after it was fitted with a footblock to the rear of the tender to aid watering, and also canvas draught screens between tender and cab.

G.W. Morrison

Plate 187: Right   On 29th July, 1964 No. 72009 *Clan Stewart* nears Dunblane heading the 09.25 Crewe—Perth express.

D. Cross

**ANGLO SCOTTISH
FROM CARLISLE**

Plate 188: *Above*   The first engine of the class, No. 72000 *Clan Buchanan* left Crewe Works in December 1951, followed by nine more during the next 3 months. The first five were shedded at Polmadie and the remaining five at Carlisle Kingmoor. One of the Polmadie engines, No. 72004 *Clan Macdonald*, is heading a Birmingham—Glasgow express at Carlisle on 3rd September, 1952.

J.P. Wilson

Plate 189: *Below*
Shortly after leaving Carlisle, No. 72007 *Clan Mackintosh* passes Kingmoor shed heading the 09.25 Crewe—Perth and Aberdeen on 10th August, 1964.

J.S. Whiteley

Plate 190: Above   The lovely upper Clyde Valley near Wandel Mill forms the setting for No. 72002 *Clan Campbell* heading a Glasgow—Blackpool relief on 14th July, 1962.
D. Cross

Plate 191: Below   Regarded by many as one of the most attractive stretches of the West Coast main line is the Lune Gorge in the Westmorland Hills. No. 72001 *Clan Cameron* races through the gorge and nears Tebay on a Manchester—Glasgow train on 7th August, 1960.

D. Cross

Plate 192: Above The Clans were similar in design to the Britannias but had a smaller boiler of 225 lb/sq in working pressure compared to the 250 lb/sq in of the Britannias. They were often criticised for poor steaming and in this picture No. 72004 *Clan Macdonald* is being helped to the summit by Fowler 2-6-4T No. 42319, having run short of steam on a Glasgow–Blackpool. 11th August, 1962.

G.W. Morrison

Plate 193: Below Polmadie Clan No. 72001 *Clan Cameron* breasts Shap Summit unassisted on the 10 coach 13.15 Manchester–Glasgow on 29th August, 1959. This engine was obviously running well and can be seen to have a full head of steam, no doubt at the expense of heavy coal consumption. The fireman will be in need of a breather on the downhill run to Penrith.

G.W. Morrison

Plate 194: Above Lifting this 12 coach Liverpool—Glasgow express unassisted to Shap Summit from Tebay is no mean feat, but the fireman appears to be having to work extremely hard. No. 72001 *Clan Cameron* is in charge on 4th August, 1960. *D. Cross*

Plate 195: Below No. 72003 *Clan Fraser* has the assistance of Fowler 2-6-4T No. 42404 for the climb from Tebay to the summit whilst in charge of an afternoon Liverpool—Glasgow. They are seen passing Greenholme on 28th July, 1960. *D. Cross*

BETWEEN DUTIES IN MANCHESTER

Plate 196: Right
The Clans were intended for the Highland Line, but their adhesive weight of only 56 tons 18 cwt was not ideal and as a result they were used mainly on Glasgow—Manchester/Liverpool trains. They were fitted with a tender identical to the type BR1 fitted to the first batch of Britannias with a capacity of 7 tons of coal and 4250 gallons of water. No. 72002 *Clan Campbell* is being watered at Newton Heath on 24th August, 1955.

B. Morrison

Plate 197: Below
Inside Bank Hall on 23rd August, 1955 is No. 72000 *Clan Buchanan* with Aspinall 1F 0-6-0T No. 51546 and Kitson 0F 0-4-0ST No. 47002 for company.

B. Morrison

CLAN MACDONALD CALLS AT PENRITH

Plates 198 and 199   On 3rd September, 1952, when only about 7 months old, No. 72004 of Polmadie pauses for passengers whilst heading the 13.45 Glasgow—Liverpool. After a stop of a few minutes it is seen accelerating away from the station with the former CK & P bay for Keswick on the left hand side of the picture.

Both J.P. Wilson

Plate 200: Above   On the 11th August, 1964 No. 72009 *Clan Stewart* makes an all out effort on the nine coach 09.25 Crewe—Perth. Northbound trains were faced with almost ten miles of climbing from Beattock station to the summit on gradients between 1 in 88 and 1 in 69 and often took banking assistance.   *J.S. Whiteley*

Plate 201: Above Right   No. 72001 *Clan Cameron* has the assistance of a banker on 24th April, 1962 whilst heading a down mixed freight. The pair are seen near Auchencastle, still with a long way to go to the summit.

J.S. Whiteley

Plate 202: Bottom Right   Beattock Summit is 1015 feet above sea level, but the climb faced by southbound trains is not as severe as for northbound trains. On 14th July, 1962 No. 72000 *Clan Buchanan* breasts the summit heading an up express.   *G.W. Morrison*

FISH AT STIRLING

Plate 203: Right
The Clans were often seen on up fish traffic from Perth and on 24th August, 1964 No. 72007 *Clan Mackintosh* pauses on the 16.45 from Perth.

J.S. Whiteley

Plate 204: Below
In this picture of the same train departing from Stirling, the foot-block added to the rear of the tender to aid watering can clearly be seen. By this date only the King-moor Clans were left because at the end of 1962 the Scottish Region had withdrawn all the Polmadie Clans in their efforts to eliminate express steam locomotives as quickly as possible.

J.S. Whiteley

Plate 205: *Above*   No. 72009 *Clan Stewart* is on home ground at Carlisle Kingmoor alongside 'Coronation' Pacific No. 46226 *Duchess of Norfolk* which certainly looks much more powerful by comparison. 6th April, 1962.

G.W. Morrison

SHED PARTNERS

Plate 206: *Below*   At Leeds Holbeck on 21st August, 1961 No. 72006 *Clan Mackenzie* of Kingmoor stands behind BR class 5 4-6-0 No. 73003 of Bristol.

G.W. Morrison

THE WAVERLEY

Plate 207: *Above*   A very dirty No. 72009 *Clan Stewart* passes Marley Junction, near Keighley on 26th May, 1961 heading the down train.   *G.W. Morrison*

Plate 208: *Below*   The 'Waverley' ran between St. Pancras and Edinburgh Waverley, and in the early 1960s for a period, Clans were to be seen on the train between Leeds and Carlisle. No. 72008 *Clan Macleod* is leaving Leeds City on 12th May, 1961 on the start of its journey to Carlisle.
                                                        G.W. Morrison

FREIGHT DUTIES

Plate 209: *Above*
On 22nd August, 1964 No. 72008
Clan Macleod has just emerged
from Moncrief Tunnel at Hilton
Junction, Perth, whilst heading an
up fish train.

J.S. Whiteley

Plate 210: *Right*
No. 72007 *Clan Mackintosh* makes
a vigorous departure from Leeds at
Whitehall Junction on a Carlisle
train in February, 1961.

J.S. Whiteley

Plate 211: *Above*   The summit of the former Glasgow and South Western main line between Kilmarnock and Dumfries is at Polquhap, near New Cumnock. No. 72006 *Clan Mackenzie* is emerging from Blackfaulds cutting on the approach to the summit heading an Ayr–Carlisle mail on 27th May, 1963.   *D. Cross*

IN SOUTH WEST SCOTLAND

Plate 212: *Below*   Another picture taken on the Nith Valley line shows No. 72007 *Clan Mackintosh* nearing Garrochburn Sidings on the 05.30 Glasgow St. Enoch–Carlisle train in July 1964.   *D. Cross*

Plate 213: *Above* The wild scenery of Galloway forms a superb setting for this picture of No. 72007 (*Clan Mackintosh*) climbing from the Big Water of Fleet Viaduct to Gatehouse of Fleet on the Dumfries—Stranraer line on 30th May, 1965. It is heading a troop special from Woodburn, in Northumberland, to Stranraer.   *D. Cross*

Plate 214: *Below* No. 72007 (*Clan Mackintosh*) is at Ayr heading a Stranraer—Newcastle train on 7th August, 1965, only a few months before being withdrawn. Unlike the Britannias, not all the Clans latterly ran without nameplates.
                                                                D. Cross

Plate 215: Above   On 27th July, 1964 No. 72007 *Clan Mackintosh* passes Annbank, not far from Ayr, heading a Manchester—Largs excursion.   *D. Cross*

Plate 216: Below   A fine picture of No. 72009 *Clan Stewart* working hard at Garrochburn heading a heavy return Ardrossan—Halifax excursion on 22nd June, 1963.   *D. Cross*

CLAN MACKINTOSH
IN LANCASHIRE

Plate 217: *Above*   No. 72007 *Clan Mackintosh* approaches Salwick, between Preston and Blackpool whilst heading an excursion to Blackpool Illuminations on 21st September, 1963.   *G.W. Morrison*

Plate 218: *Below*   No. 72007 is seen on 23rd May, 1964 heading an RCTS special in a very unusual setting, Lancaster Old Goods Yard.   *G.W. Morrison*

IN SERVICE . . .

Plate 219: *Above* An attractive study of Kingmoor engine No. 72005 *Clan Macgregor* at Perth.

G.W. Morrison

OUT OF SERVICE . . .

Plate 220: Below The Polmadie engines were the first to be withdrawn, all in December 1962. The Kingmoor engines were gradually withdrawn from service from April 1965 as they became due for repairs, and No. 72006 *Clan Mackenzie* was the last one to go in May 1966. Several Clans ended their days at Darlington, and No. 72001 (*Clan Cameron*) is seen there awaiting cutting up on 12th October, 1963, almost one year after being withdrawn from service.

G.W. Morrison